FLAWLESS

Looking for Stardom…finding Jesus

Victoria *Kulczycki*

Kingdom Publishers

www.kingdompublishers.co.uk

Flawless

ISBN: 978-1-913247-11-9

1st Edition by Kingdom Publishers
Kingdom Publishers
London, UK.

Definition: adjective, Flawless

1) without any imperfections or defects; perfect

2) synonyms: perfect, without blemish, unblemished, unmarked, unimpaired

Dedication

To Elsie and Edward, praying you'll read
this one day...

Contents

Foreward

B efore I even wrote a word of this book, I asked family members and friends whether I should write it. The reasons I was unsure included; would people really want to hear about my life? My Christian conversion? Would they want to hear the details (often uncomfortable) of my life? My admissions, thoughts, deepest secrets? Was it a secret vanity project? Did I just want praise and adoration? Was I trying to detract from Jesus and heap some sort of value upon myself?

The answer to all of the above is truly this; I want to glorify God. Our great, almighty, loving God who took my hard, stubborn, worldly, atheistic heart and changed it through the blood of His son, the Lord Jesus Christ. Praise be to my King.

Prologue

I love those films that start at the end and then whizz back in time so we can follow the journey of how they got there. Well, I'm not quite at the end, but I am in the present, sitting on the second to back row of church, it's an evening service (my husband is kindly putting the kids to bed) and we've just sung one of my favourite hymns, And Can It Be by Charles Wesley. A classic! My heart pounding in my chest as we join together to sing the lines; *Bold I approach the eternal throne, And claim the crown, through Christ my own!*

Bold. It's a funny word. I always pronounce it wrong. I speak it as if I'm saying bald, as in hairless. But in this case, I never pronounce it wrong, because it actually means something, something great; the ability to be BOLD in the presence of a Holy God. And I can only be BOLD in Christ, for I have nothing without Him, he is my confidence, my assurance and my saviour. And the crown referred to in that wonderful hymn is, the crown of the King, the Lord Jesus, who reigns, the King who was put to death on a cross, the King who rose from the dead, the King who lives and who will come again to claim his people.

So that's where I am, sitting down, listening to the preacher speak faithfully from the Bible, pleased to be alongside my brothers and sisters In Christ who are sitting listening with me. I'm precisely where God wants me to be. So, therefore I must trust that God has always had me precisely where he wanted me and will use my testimony and the life he allowed me to live, in order to glorify Himself, which is the perfect introduction to Part One, which I will call My Old Life. Anyone with a nervous disposition should look away now...

PART ONE

My Old Life

Chapter 1
School Days

Just like in Bill Bryson's A Short History of Nearly Everything, I am going to have to skim over some parts of my childhood and adolescence just so that we are not here all day.

I was born in November, 1982, the same year Michael Jackson released his Thriller album, Channel 4 was launched, the film E.T came out and everyone was listening to The jam or The Human League. I was born in Bradford, at the BRI to Caroline and James Smith. We lived in Wrose, in the first house mum and dad bought after they got married, it was perched on a steep hill with wonderful views over Shipley. My brother Alexander came along twenty months later and we moved to Baildon, a small village on the outskirts of Bradford nicely nestled on the edge of the Moors, and that's where I spent my childhood.

It was a lovely childhood; one of those typical 80's/90's ones that meant being outside all the time, playing in woods, building dens, climbing trees and fighting with sticks. Before the corruption of mobile phones and computers. I had a group of boys as friends from about 2 years old, which resulted in me being a tom boy. I would race around, red faced, riding my bike, staying out late and having fun. Our family holidays consisted of going abroad twice a year, sometimes three times, always to the same place; Cala Galdana in Menorca. We were comfortable, my dad worked hard as a sales rep and my mum worked as a child minder and looked after me and my brother. *I want to add something here and its not just lip service – my parents really are great people, my mum is a patient, loving, warm person, who would do anything to help anyone and my dad is everything you would want in a dad, a strong, present character who was always there for me; he's the only person in the world that when I'm in a car with, I can close my eyes, trusting he has everything under control. My dad has always been my safety net, and my mum; my best friend. None of us believed in God, God was rarely mentioned in my childhood, I went to a Church of England school but so did plenty of kids '*back then*.' We heard the odd Bible story and did a funny *Christingle* thing once a year, where you stick some jelly tots on a stick, pierce the skin of an orange, dig out its pulp and replace with a candle, tie a ribbon around the middle and walk very slowly down the center aisle of a church, in this case St John's Parish Church in Baildon. It was fun but I didn't have a clue what it meant.

I excelled at sport, I was always a really fast sprinter, which pleased my dad, and I won first place at most sports days until a girl named Alexa, my arch enemy, became faster, then I was always second and not happy being second, I stopped altogether. By the time I got to high school I barely made forth or fifth place. I was quite a good swimmer, again following in the footsteps of my athletic dad, but I was never going to be Olympic standard, so I probably gave up not long after starting. Academically, I was pretty useless, in fact, I think I've got cleverer as I've got older, but I think that's the case for most people. I loved books, I've always been a big reader, in fact I remember queuing up for my free little copy of the New Testament when I was about eight, they were giving them out at school, I wanted one so badly and felt elated once it was safely in my hands. Its cover was made from some sort of bendy red plastic and I can still remember its smell now, all synthetic and sickly. Never read it though, it just felt nice to have on my bookshelf. I'd felt the same about a copy of Doctor Dolittle and The Famous Five.

So, between the years of 1-13 I kind of sailed through, distinctly average at school, so no great promise, but I wasn't bullied, I didn't bully anyone and generally got on with it. On entering my teen years, a few things started to go a bit wrong. I developed *really bad* skin, as in really bad. As in hospital visits and dermatologist - bad. The acne was red and sore and all over my face, back and chest. I was so mortified at the raised crimson pimples on my face and neck that I used to wear thick, gloopy foundation, not too dissimilar to theatrical stage makeup, full coverage, everyday, for school. To make matters worse and to encourage the hurtful jibes I'd receive, the orthodontist fitted me with blue coloured train-track braces and I had my long hair permed and dyed purple. I was an absolute state! I remember on one particular non-uniform day, wearing a Guns and Roses t-shirt with flared jeans and trainers. Oh and my eyebrows met in the middle.

I was put on medication for my acne, first Roaccutane, a serious and potent drug that I believe has now been taken off the market. I was only fifteen and had to do a pregnancy test as routine due to the destructive nature of the drug on a potential unborn child. Which was mortifying. I took the drug for a few months under medical supervision, it kind of worked, sucking every last drop of moisture from my skin so grease couldn't sit and clog the pores, but due to the lack of moisture, my skin cracked and bled, my lips split and bled. Once I came off it, the acne returned, as bad as it had been before. Great. Various medications followed but none worked, in the end I guessed it was my skin and my great hurdle in life.

This happening to me had a huge impact on the course of my life.

I would sit in front of the mirror and pretend I was a beautiful actress - the most beautiful actress. Obviously I wasn't beautiful, I was a mess; my face was caked in thick orange sludge, my eyes were darkened with lashings of mascara and liner and my lips were red, always red and I was a child. I'd plucked my eyebrows so they each boasted about seven hairs, which forced me to draw them on, in a color that didn't match my purple hair. The orange line of foundation tracked my jaw then stopped, so I was different colours. I wanted to cry all the time because looks are that important, or at least, they are to a teenage girl who was starting to lose her confidence.

I avoided joining in with any sort of outdoor activity, because my face and the mismatching skin colours looked really bad in natural light and people could be really cruel. I would retreat back into my room, to the mirror, where I accepted awards for my stunning on screen work, my best actress nominations. I recall one of my stage names was Donna Monero (Donna – because I thought it was a cool name and Monero - because it was John Travolta's character's name in Saturday Night Fever and I liked it)

So there I was; sixteen years old, no date to the May Ball because I was a pizza faced, greasy haired, goofy adolescent. But my mum thought I was beautiful. It's funny what your motivations are as a teenager. Unless you are really academically gifted or driven, it all comes down to looks and boys and who had the newest Nike Air Max trainers and the shortest skirt. Again, it would be helpful to note, I never considered God once, I didn't even believe I was created, I believed what was taught in school, something about an explosion, dinosaurs and men been apes millions or billions (or trillions) of years ago. Anyway, none of that mattered, all I really knew was that I was alive, and life was tough.

At sixteen I decided something that my husband still finds funny to this day. I turned to my mum and said (remember I'm sixteen) 'I want to be a dancer.' I said it through brace laden teeth, with a slight lisp. Mum, forever the optimist, took me to go see Fame the musical and that confirmed my choice. I was going to be a dancer and perhaps turn into an actress, I would work firstly on stage then be a actress on the silver screen. Those awards would be mine.

I auditioned for the Northern School of Contemporary Dance in Leeds and gained a place on the foundation course. There I was; full face caked in orange foundation, no eyebrows, greasy long hair wound into a bun and a lilac coloured unitard. Teachers would say things like, 'you'll have to work extra hard to improve your muscle tone, especially because you are pear shaped.'

Great. Pear shaped. I could add that to my list of shortcomings. I tried to ignore when looking in the mirror. A year later I auditioned and won a place on the degree course. I completed my degree in summer 2003 with a two/one BA hons. In that time, I'd worked hard physically, I'd grown somewhat in confidence and my spots were almost gone (or very faint) So I modeled for a Vidal Sassoon fashion show which meant I had to have all my hair cut off. Boy short. Military short. It looked good. For years I had hidden beneath a fountain of gothic dark, greasy hair, parted in the middle and hanging closely over my face to limit the amount of skin visible.

Now I was free. Liberated. The burden of hiding was gone.

I was twenty years old when I moved to London.

Chapter 2
The Streets Aren't Paved with Gold

My parents didn't want me to go to London. Why would any parent want their daughter to move to a city that gobbled you up and spat you out? My mum was emotional about it but it was my dad that was really against the idea. I remember standing on the platform at Leeds, my rucksack on my back, a mirror and a duvet strapped to it. That's all. I didn't have anything else. I wanted to tell them, it's going to be ok! I'm going to be in movies! I'll buy you a huge house in Ilkley with my first acting cheque!

I boarded the train and waved goodbye. How grown up I was! A young woman, with everything she owned on her back, cropped hair, slim figure and clear skin, a book wedged beneath my arm to make me look worldly and clever. I would succeed now. Nothing would stop me. I was determined to show everyone. I was determined to get as far away from Bradford as possible. London, at 203 miles away, was pretty far and I needed an actual physical distance to prove to myself that I'd achieved something.

My first home was a dirty room in a flat share of seven people, mostly drag queens who went by the name Paul and Steve and Gary during the day and Vanilla Lush, Candy Crush and Betty Boo by night. The flat was in one of the most dangerous estates in South London that I'd found advertised in Loot newspaper, you basically see a room advertised, call the number and if you'd got there first then you could move in before the day was out. No checks. No references. You don't know who you'll be living with. So the room I had bagged first was on the Aylesbury Estate, a large council built estate, which resembled a large collection of run down, grisly tombs. It was all I could afford at the time, my room costing £80 per week for an eight foot by eight foot square and one lockable cupboard in a mucky kitchen.

The best way to describe the estate is found here, off the creationtrust.org website;

"Problems with the building began almost the moment the construction was complete. Leaks and floods, problems with the lifts and vermin have been ongoing issues for years.

Over the decades, crime and the fear of crime, has also been a major concern for residents. However, in the major headline grabbing incidents that have taken place on the estate, the perpetrators were not actually residents of the Aylesbury estate, but had found the architecture of the area conducive to carrying out their crimes."

I'm not being snobby, I simply want to highlight how different my living experience was in London compared with my family home up north. Obviously, mum and dad weren't pleased and I had to grow up fast. Life wasn't cushy and easy anymore. I had to be sensible and vigilant. My job handing out programs in the west end theatres saw me arriving back at the estate late at night, and, having braved the night bus, the next hurdle was to run, literally run, from the bus stop to my second floor flat, which I shared with strangers. Many times I was chased. Usually by men. Drunk men.

Also, the majority of people were black on the estate, which meant I stood out as a minority and that brought a fair share of unwanted attention.

I earned approximately £150 per week, which meant I could afford my rent, my bus pass, my phone bill and a packet of cigarettes. No food. So I slimed down to a size eight, which pleased the agent I had managed to get. I had joined an agency as an actress (untrained) and not a dancer. I had to face facts, there were better dancers than me, but that £9,000 on my degree hadn't gone completely to waste, I could now stand up straight and point my toes when I needed to.

But auditions didn't come as easy as I'd thought they would. I would turn up, rehearse my lines, walk into the audition room and many a time before I'd even opened my mouth, they would shout 'No!' 'Next!' Charming! It did start to wear me down after a while, but I kept on, determined to bag at least one acting job to tell mum and dad about. But a year went by. Then two years. Nothing. I did daily dance classes to keep in the loop at Pineapple Dance Studios and worked in the evenings at Her Majesty's Theatre and the Theatre Royal Drury Lane. I was happy. Turned out I had a talent for selling programs and interval ice creams. Plus I got to watch a host of amazing plays and musicals, which only confirmed my ambitions of becoming an actress.

Famous people passed by my seating section almost every night, acting heroes. I was promoted to a Red Coat, which was one of Andrew Lloyd Webber's VIP hosts and I personally looked after Prince Charles and Camilla Parker Bowles, Boris Yeltzin, Pierce Brosnan, Helen Mirren, and many more. Life on the outside was good.

But inside I was yearning for more. I wanted fame! I wanted people to be in awe of me! It's so hard to admit now, because its coming from a person I no longer know, but that was the kind of determination required to make it in such a fickle and shallow business. And scraping the barrel of one's pride was what I was willing to do.

After two years of not nailing one audition. I finally got a call from my agent. I'd got one! I'd got the job! A 'Snack a Jacks' television commercial, filming in Cape Town, South Africa! This was it! The start! I called mum and dad in tears, I'd got the job! Over and above loads of other girls!

But something else was happening. Something that didn't spark concern at first but grew, like a fungus, spreading, requiring my attention, needing addressing;

I was beginning to feel a hole forming in my gut, it was unexplainable at first, it was an emptiness, like a void but a tangible void, something I could feel but couldn't quite put into words.

So I began to fill it with stuff. I flew to Cape Town and filmed the advert. I stayed at a posh hotel in Camps Bay and flew business class. I felt like a real star. Everything was paid for! On the flight I had one of those pods to sleep in, my food was served on actual plates and I got a glass of prosecco once I was seated and settled in. I had money in the form of per diams, which basically meant you get a load of cash and can spend as much as you like per day. I even got to visit Johannesburg briefly before I left the country, a place I'd been interested in for years. And so a flurry of TV commercials followed due to a boost in my confidence; I filmed in Hungary, Israel, South Africa and London, filming adverts for Samsung,

Channel 4, DFS, Kotex etc. I was on my way. The void would definitely go soon.

I stayed out late at night, drinking in a pub opposite the Theatre Royal with my friends well into the early hours and was now living in a top floor flat in Brixton with a girl called Nicola who I'd met through a friend. The seventeen floors up were best reached by a cranky old lift that you just hoped and prayed the council had got round to servicing in the last decade. Plus it stank of cannabis, so by the time you reached the top floor, you were high as a kite. The living situation, however, was much better than before, but there was one annoying thing Nicola did almost every night, when I rolled in from the night bus, half drunk and shattered.

She read me stories from the Bible.

Nicola was a Christian, she attended a Gospel Church in Brixton and absolutely belonged to the Lord. She would make me sit on the couch, whilst she told me about God. About Jesus Christ.

Who? I remember thinking.

I didn't have time for this, plus I was looking into Buddhism, an easygoing religion that didn't require anything from me and I liked Yoga and all the spiritual jargon that went with it. I'd even bought some yoga pants, a mat and a small handbook 'A Beginners guide to Buddhism.' So I was all set, thank you.

Nicola spoke of the Kingdom of Heaven.

I wanted to giggle. Fancy anyone, in this day in age, still believing in the God of the Bible? Those stories were old. So much had happened in the world since. It was just a metaphor anyhow, and a collection of rules probably put together to spoil everybody's fun.

I don't recall her actually explaining the Gospel of Christ to me, she probably did, but I wasn't listening, I was probably thinking about what I was going to wear the next day.

Chapter 3
Transatlantic Dreams

The roll I was on continued. I was successful and totally full of myself. Once I turned twenty three in 2005, I'd hit my stride. I was bagging almost every audition I went into to. I was filming a lot during the day and still hanging out with my *out of work/resting* actor friends in the evening at the theatre, handing out programs and larking around. It wouldn't be long before I got a movie or a prominent television role. I felt sure of it.

I had money when a job got paid. Then I had nothing again. But it didn't matter, because I was on my way. I was thin (Thanks to a diet of cigarettes, black coffee and the odd carrot stick) and pretty (so people said) and that was a winning combination. I would strut around Leicester Square, pretending to be famous, pulling my collar up high to hide my face, but secretly knowing that people would look, whose the girl hiding beneath her coat? The one with the red lips and pink cheeks? I was totally self- absorbed. I likened myself to a female James Dean (don't know why) I watched all his movies (all 3) and sat reading scripts and plays, pretending to be deep in thought, I even bought some clear lensed glasses and a stripy t-shirt.

I had boyfriends. Plenty. I was popular. Popular and aloof.

The void was still there. It remained there when my life took an even more impressive turn in February 2006, when I auditioned for an American Television Show featuring Gene Simmons from the glam rock band, KISS. It was called Gene Simmons Family Jewels and I was auditioning for the part of girlfriend to Nick Simmons, Gene's son. I didn't fit the required look, my agent sent me despite the audition call being for tall blonde girls for the part but it didn't matter, I nailed the audition.

My agent called me an hour later to tell me I'd got the job but she needn't have, I already knew I'd got it the moment my audition finished and the producers just stared at me, impressed. I'd learnt to interpret the look on people's faces and used to bet my friends how long it would take for them to confirm I had the job! It'll please you to know that I cringe thinking back on these memories. Cringe at the person I was. It's so embarrassing it's tragic.

The self-obsession was eating me up, I was mistreating my body physically in many ways, filling my head with new age nonsense, narcissism, self-adoration and ambition. I wanted to achieve something. I wanted fame and glory. I kept telling myself how all the experiences I had in life wouldn't affect me long term, I was normal, it was normal behavior, to smoke and go out with boys and drink too much so you vomit in the toilets of clubs, fall asleep over the toilet rim, wake up when the cleaners came in and stumbled to the night bus. I took slimming tablets when I felt fat and hung out with my drag queen friends on Old Compton Street, often jumping up onto the podiums and dancing to cheers and applause, caught up in the hysteria of a hedonistic life.

None of this would haunt me, damage me or leave scars, why would it? This was what life was all about – Carpe Diam! Seize the day! Don't regret the things you do, just the things you didn't do! Life's too short! You could die tomorrow! Make it count!

My agent called one morning to say I'd got the part in Gene Simmons Family Jewels television show. We would be filming in London initially, Chelsea. So I went along, filmed my scenes and enjoyed being part of the crazy show. Then, a few months later and supposedly just after Season 2 of the show had aired in the United States, I was contacted by the producers. Would I like to fly over to Los Angeles and film some episodes for Season 3?

Yes please! I was over the moon! I called mum and dad, they were excited for me. I packed my bags and was on an Air New Zealand flight to LAX within days. This was it. Definitely it. I was going to be a famous actress. My Oscar was almost in sight!

When I landed in LA, I was assigned a driver, my personal driver, who I convinced to drive me around the sights before taking me to my hotel, a suite at the Hilton Beverly Hills. Hollywood! I was in Hollywood! I had to see the sign, up close. I wanted to see Graumans Chinese

Theatre, the Hollywood walk of fame and Santa Monica beach! I ran up and down Rodeo Drive (as my hotel was opposite) I was convinced it wouldn't be long now before a casting director noticed me walking down the street, hanging out at the beach and cast me as the new, young starlet in their movies. How naïve I was. Naïve and ambitious.

We filmed daily. I hung out at Gene Simmons' Hollywood home, in his kitchen, playing with his dogs and discussing British music. We filmed in various locations around LA, I was miked up constantly as it was scripted, reality television. It was long days, beginning at 6am and ending at 8pm, it was more the setting up for shots that took a long time, and filming the same scenes over and over again until they were perfect. I would go for drinks in Hollywood with the production team afterward and they convinced me to stay in Los Angeles, they said I had a great 'look' and could make it in the industry if I worked hard. After filming was over I tore up my return ticket and stayed in LA, my agent said she'd get me film auditions or television auditions through her Los Angeles counterpart. Things were going perfectly.

I'd become good friends with my driver and his mates, turned out they were in a band and were pretty good. So I began to carve out a new life, with new friends. It became one long, endless party.

Sitting on Santa Monica Beach one evening, the sun setting, the lifeguard towers darkening, the beach from the hit 90's show Baywatch, only a few miles down the coast, I stared up at the sky. One of my friends was close by, playing guitar but I couldn't really hear the music. It was a strange moment, I remember it clearly, because I believe it was the first moment God had prodded me.

The emptiness was still there, in my gut. Bigger and more painful than it had been before. It throbbed and hurt, knotted and twisted and threatened to turn me inside out. I still wasn't certain what it was. Perhaps it was the beginnings of a mental illness? Depression? Perhaps my brain had been damaged by the alcohol and nicotine?

I sat there, sand between my toes, the sun disappearing over the horizon and contemplated my life. Surely I should be happy? This was the dream! I was living my dream! I'd made it!

I shrugged it off again. After all, life was hard, I had to believe in myself, nobody else was going to look after me, I was a young woman at the mercy of a tough business, it required a strong will, confidence and focus. Perhaps I was simply feeling the pressure. It took a great deal of determination to be successful.

Two years passed. Thanks to a temporary visitor permit visa (which has since been revised) I had to leave the country every few months and return home, only to board a flight to the USA again not long after. I decided, in a landmark decision, to stop acting. I was twenty five years old, bored with acting, confused by the void in my heart and had a fistful of money from my Gene Simmons stint. So I joined my newly acquired American friends, who were in a band called Upshot and we left California in a battered old Chrysler, to travel across the country, driving through Arizona, New Mexico, Texas, Oklahoma, Arkansas, Tennessee, Kentucky and finally arriving in Ohio, our destination.

Life was still a party. I tagged along with the band, partied at night, lived in a barn style house in Loveland, Ohio and basically did everything I could to ignore the painful void as it grew in its intensity. It became so strong that I felt as though I had little choice in my next decision.

I was twenty seven years old when I called it quits and bought a ticket home.

Chapter 4
Coming Home

Returning home wasn't easy. I flew from Chicago Airport, on a BA flight bound for Manchester, UK. Mum and dad still lived in the house I grew up in, in Baildon and came to the airport to pick me up one Thursday morning. My brother, thankfully, was still at home and I made every attempt to settle back in. Back in to normal, everyday life. It had been my decision to come home, to give up acting and although I was happy with my choice, I wasn't quite sure where I fitted in.

Practically, there were things I needed to do to adjust smoothly, I didn't drive and the buses were every half an hour unlike London buses, so I had to learn to drive ASAP, the other was that I needed a job, because I had no money left. In the following months I started part time work at Salts Mill, in Saltaire, working the till and restocking David Hockney postcards. It wasn't much money but it eased me back into a normal existence, which I was finding difficult.

When my temporary contract at Salts Mill was up, I increased my skillset to manning reception at the local Ramada Jarvis Hotel, full time. It never ceased to surprise me when people offered me a job off the back of a CV that says all I'm qualified to do is dance and act! Ha! Never the less, A year or so later, I left the hotel and began to manage a holistic, chiropractic clinic on the outskirts of Leeds. I was simply existing at this point, muddling through, being just like everyone else. I would go out clubbing every weekend, drink, often throw up, (once in a friend's car which was mortifying) and worked a respectable 9-5 job that paid poorly but kept me busy. I was a little bit like a zombie, I wasn't sure what my plan was, my purpose, I didn't know what I wanted to do anymore and the worst thing was, I'd stopped caring. I lived for the Now, the Present.

*I just wanted to add here that it is obvious from where I am now, in the present, that the twisting journey I was on, seemingly chaotic and spontaneous, was in fact a perfectly manicured plan by God. God allowed me twenty eight years of winding my way around the world, on a path that seemed to lead absolutely nowhere, before finally meeting me where I was.

His plan was perfect and it would Glorify Him. It would be as I was managing the clinic in Leeds that I would hear the Gospel of Jesus Christ, and respond.

PART TWO
New Life

Chapter 5
Hearing the Truth

Imagine this; you are a successful person in many ways, you've accomplished many things that people find fascinating and impressive, you are considered good at your present job and are trusted in the running of an entire clinic of professionals. You have friends, hang out in Gay Bars every weekend, wear 6/7 inch heels and have an attitude that screams *I don't care!* Imagine you are confrontational, not just confident, but happy to pull people up on things, to stand your ground, even finding yourself the instigator of arguments. Imagine that your misuse of alcohol gave you an extra confidence to do this. Imagine that your language is appalling, curse words and blasphemy peppering every conversation. Imagine that you don't believe in God. You are an atheist and happy to tell people as much. Imagine that the last book you downloaded on your Kindle before hearing something that would change your life forever, was Darwin's Origins of Species (research material for a story I was writing) Imagine that person, sitting behind a desk, primed for disagreement, like a coiled spring, suddenly hears that they are a SINNER. If they are not with God, then they are *against* Him. That they are going to hell.

Imagine that.

Well that's exactly what happened. Let's rewind a little.

A man walks in to the clinic, his name is Jon, he was a rep for a company who was to have some dealings with our company. I was polite and welcomed him in. He seemed like a gentle sort, friendly and smiley, I wasn't actually used to seeing people that happy. Didn't think to ask what it was that made him so…cheerful.

He didn't look over at me, just kept to the job in hand, meeting with my boss to discuss some matter. I assumed he was homosexual. That's how self obsessed I'd become, presuming that if a male didn't look at me for longer than five seconds, then he must be gay. I decided on one last tactic, and it's a tale my husband loves to tell when he's in front of a crowd, it went down particularly well at our wedding reception in fact. The tactic was, he'd parked in our company car park and after the meeting, he went back to his car to makes some calls, so I whipped around the side of the building and locked the gate, so he wouldn't be able to leave, he'd have to come and find me first and ask if I could open the gate. Hilarious, but embarrassing looking back. So yeah, he came and asked politely, I opened it and that was that.

We exchanged pleasantries and went about our day. I didn't hear from him again for another couple of months when our paths crossed again due to work. I'd decided. I would ask the shy boy out for a drink.

He didn't drink, he told me.

'Didn't drink?' I asked, appalled.

'No, I prefer Shloer.' He replied.

'Ok, coffee then?'

'Can't.' he said.

Hmmm, this was strange, unfamiliar ground.

'Why not?'

'I'm a committed Christian.' he replied, 'I belong to Christ, it wouldn't be right to meet with you.'

'Belonged to Christ?'

'Yes, I belong to Christ.'

This was weird.

Apart from Nicola from the Brixton flat, I'd never met someone who *belonged to Christ* before. How can you *belong* to someone anyway?

So we didn't meet up. Instead he dismissed a relationship and chose to tell me about Jesus.

It might help at this time, to learn what I already knew about Jesus;

He was born in a stable, in Bethlehem. Three wise men brought him gifts, I'm fairly certain they rode on camels and the world rejoiced at his birth. The Messiah was born. Although I wasn't sure what 'Messiah' meant. Then Jesus became a carpenter and led a quiet life, before doing a few miracles, like walking on water etc, only to die on a cross, his body put in a cave and a few days later the cave was found empty.

But what did that story have to do with me?

I'd heard the word Sin too, banded around but assumed it related to horrid acts like murder, rape, extra marital affairs, theft and such like. I didn't think for a moment it would be of concern to someone like me, a normal person, just muddling through life.

I asked him if he read the Bible. He answered yes, daily. I found that strange, I didn't know much about the Bible, only that it was very old, probably full of fables, old fashioned law, dated and legalistic rules for living life. God would feature as some sort of dictator and scary judge and when people didn't agree or live by his rules, they felt the wrath of His anger?

I was guessing. I was drawing on worldly perception and popular culture to build my own picture.

So I politely said I would read an email he was preparing to send, that contained the testimony of his late dad, Edward, and a video testimony of Ian McCormac (a young man from New Zealand, an atheist, who was stung by five Box Jellyfish whilst diving in Creole and found himself in God's presence.) Also bible verses and the clear Gospel message.

This was how I understood it all as I read:

I was a SINNER before a Holy God.

A sinner by birth, by nature. We all are. And it's that sin that separates us from a relationship and closeness with God. Because he is TOTALLY good and therefore cannot have a relationship with someone marred by sin. That sin has to be obliterated.

He created me for a relationship, I am His child, His creation, yet I refused to acknowledged it, I went about my life ignoring Him, blissfully unaware of the lengths He went to, to forgive me. God is real. Judgment is real. Heaven and Hell are real. Jesus Christ was put on this earth, born of a woman but fully God, to live the life that I could never live. Then he died. He had to die. God, being a just and perfect God, had to punish sin. So Jesus took the sins of the world upon His shoulders, because he loved us so much. At the CROSS God's wrath was appeased. He was satisfied. The curse was broken. Jesus was raised from the dead. He now reigns at God's right hand. He is the King of the world and will return again to gather His people, to take them into paradise with Him, through a narrow gate, to a new heaven and a new earth. He is The Way.

Whoa.

That's a mind blowing Truth to be faced with and once you've heard it, its really difficult to shake off. And so it should be; its life giving, it's a spiritual defibrillator for a flat-lining heart. It's love in its purest form. Love we can only see glimpses and shadows of on this earth. When I heard that, the seconds and minutes that followed involved me trying to ignore it, shrug it off as something spiritual and other-worldly, not meant for me but for those crazy people who take religion really seriously.

Yet I couldn't shake it off.

The emptiness inside me, the void, the questions as to why we are here, our purpose, how we are supposed to live our lives, what happens at the end and is their a higher power in this world or are we on our own, seemed to radiate through my body. Every cell was awakened and fizzing.

But becoming a Christian would compromise my worldly views wouldn't it? As a non-Christian person, I was free, liberal, forward thinking, open-minded, happy, unrestrained, inclusive of everyone. But that was the problem. I wasn't free. I never had been. If I didn't belong to God, then I was on the opposite team and if God is goodness and light then the other team was darkness and evil. There isn't a box in the middle for those who simply don't care, who shrug their shoulders, who remain agnostic.

I am going to use Bible verses from the book of Romans here to emphasize the point;

Romans 3:23 For all have sinned and fall short of the glory of God.

Romans 6:23 For the wages of sin is death, but the free gift of God is eternal life in Christ Jesus our Lord.

Romans 10:9-10 If you confess with your mouth that Jesus is Lord and believe in your heart that God raised him from the dead, you will be saved. For with the heart one believes and is justified, and with the mouth one confesses and is saved.

Romans 3:10-11 None is righteous, no, not one; no one understands, no one seeks for God.

It might also be helpful to know, I hate being told what to do. So I hated all this at first. That was one of my first reactions. I had often defied authority and used to think I knew best. So to be faced with these truths angered me. They choked me. They made me want to lash out; Christians were just pious, hypocrites, old fashioned, they think they're above moral and worldly issues, they are weird, spend their time reading a dusty old tome, are not very modern, certainly not 'cool' they are homophobic and sexist. I could go on.

I always had feminist values probably resulting from the fact I'd achieved a lot on my own; survived living in bad areas, survived on very little money, was educated and could stand up for myself, I had ideas, opinions and things to say. I'm happy to open my own door, and stand up on the tube, thank you very much. I had a view that women in the bible were downtrodden, subservient, quiet, compliant, seen and not heard types. That definitely wasn't for me then.

So you see, faced with all of that, and with the part of my brain bubbling away with the realization that I had a Creator, to which I was a natural enemy and needed Jesus, the Risen Lord, I fell back on to my bed and stared at the ceiling, aghast.

Chapter 6
Responding

Hours passed. I assumed I was lucid dreaming when before my eyes hovered the Lord's Prayer on some sort of wooden plinth, the words etched in gold. I recalled it from my childhood, from my years at a Church of England school and I clung to it. That was how I was going to pray to God, I would recite it over and over again. It was a strange night, a night of prayer (never prayed before this night) a night of seeing my sin in startling, high definition. Years of ignoring my creator danced before me, bright, gaudy and corrupt. I recalled all the hatred I felt for people, the angst at the state of my life, the self indulgence, the obsession and the uncertainty of who I was, it all contributed to a mountain of sin that separated me from a Holy God. In myself, I had no identity, I was a hollow shell of someone who had journeyed so far and achieved childhood dreams only to find that there was no pot of gold at the end of the rainbow, no treasure at the bottom of the ocean. No fulfillment.

I had lived my life as if the world revolved around me, there was nothing else, no bigger picture and now, faced with the truth, I realized that the universe did in fact, revolve around one person and that person was Jesus Christ.

The early hours were dark and solitary. I felt conflicted, I was seeing my sin for the first time and now I'd seen it, I could no longer ignore it. I'd come too far. Jesus had died for me, he'd dived in front of the bullet meant for me, and yet he lives. I felt him near. He was the bridge that I could cling to and walk across to be with my God, my Father. Another way I looked at it was this; God could have sent a King, a great king with worldly riches and glory, someone obvious, illustrious and impressive for us to follow, to show His greatness.

He sent Jesus Christ. Fully God, yet fully human, a humble man, pleased to serve others, he felt all the pain we have ever felt, rejection, ridicule, pity, shame, the list goes on. He was mocked and nailed to a cross, in front of a jeering crowd, a yelling, screaming, frenzied crowd, made up of the likes of you and me. He died a painful death, a death he knew he was going to from the moment he set foot on the earth, a death that involved him becoming Sin, and taking God's wrath. Enduring an unfathomable depth of pain when the Father turned His face away. What pain. Excruciating pain. Then death.

Then he was Glorified. He rose to life. He lives!

That's the enormous, limitless power of God and our assurance of an eternity spent in glory with Him.

I cried out for him to forgive me. To forgive me everything!

Things started to happen, a blissful unburdening.

I said sorry to God over and over, I wept for Jesus who had died that I might live, and this wonderful saviour was the person I wanted to spend my days with, spend eternity with. He was the one. God loved me enough to send His Son to die for me.

It says it plainly here in John's Gospel, chapter 3 verse 16, 'For God so loved the world, that he sent his only begotten son, that whoever believes in Him shall not perish but have eternal life.'

I accepted Jesus into my life, into my heart as Lord and saviour. I confessed it over and over again. I must have fallen asleep at some point because I woke the next morning to a lightness, a lightness I attribute to being reconciled with my maker. There are so many words I could use to describe that morning; I was happy, joyful, untroubled, unburdened, alive, vibrant, free.

The world looked different, because it was different. Before last night, I believed myself to be a random person on a random sphere of rock spinning in an endless universe. I was awakened, there was a Creator God, He created us for a relationship that we had destroyed in the early days. Destroyed by indulging in our own desires, in not respecting our maker for the brilliant, perfect, unchanging God he is. That destruction was in itself destroyed by the Lord Jesus Christ, and he now governed my world. He was the King. He owned the world, he held it all together in His hands. The bonds of evil, with which I had been bound for years had snapped and now I was free In Christ!

I was a child of God, a follower of Christ and I couldn't wait to tell people.

Chapter 7
A New Creature

Iwanted to write this chapter even though I knew that it felt more natural to plunge straight into what happened next. September 5th 2011 marked my first day on earth as a Believer, a born again believer In Christ. But, I wanted to add this chapter by way of praising the Lord.

Let's hear the words of our Lord Jesus Christ, explaining how one is born again. Embracing this scripture will bring understanding of what happened to me that night and how I was a changed person the very next day. It is critical to understand that this is a divine change in somebody, it is resurrecting a soul that was dead in its sin to new life. New life brings new senses and new understanding.

John 3 New International Version (NIV)

Jesus Teaches Nicodemus

3 Now there was a Pharisee, a man named Nicodemus who was a member of the Jewish ruling council. **2** He came to Jesus at night and said, "Rabbi, we know that you are a teacher who has come from God. For no one could perform the signs you are doing if God were not with him."

3 Jesus replied, "Very truly I tell you, no one can see the kingdom of God unless they are born again."

4 "How can someone be born when they are old?" Nicodemus asked. "Surely they cannot enter a second time into their mother's womb to be born!"

5 Jesus answered, "Very truly I tell you, no one can enter the kingdom of God unless they are born of water and the Spirit. **6** Flesh gives birth to flesh, but the Spirit gives birth to spirit. **7** You should not be surprised at my saying, 'You must be born again.' **8** The wind blows wherever it pleases. You hear its sound, but you cannot tell where it comes from or where it is going. So it is with everyone born of the Spirit."

9 "How can this be?" Nicodemus asked.

10 "You are Israel's teacher," said Jesus, "and do you not understand these things? **11** Very truly I tell you, we speak of what we know, and we testify to what we have seen, but still you people do not accept our testimony. **12** I have spoken to you of earthly things and you do not believe; how then will you believe if I speak of heavenly things? **13** No one has ever gone into heaven except the one who came from heaven—the Son of Man. **14** Just as Moses lifted up the snake in the wilderness, so the Son of Man must be lifted up, **15** that everyone who believes may have eternal life in him."

16 For God so loved the world that he gave his one and only Son, that whoever believes in him shall not perish but have eternal life. **17** For God did not send his Son into the world to condemn the world, but to save the world through him. **18** Whoever believes in him is not condemned, but whoever does not believe stands condemned already because they have not believed in the name of God's one and only Son. **19** This is the verdict: Light has come into the world, but people loved darkness instead of light because their deeds were evil. **20** Everyone who does evil hates the light, and will not come into the light for fear that their deeds will be exposed. **21** But whoever lives by the truth comes into the light, so that it may be seen plainly that what they have done has been done in the sight of God.

Amen.

Chapter 8

Church on the Green

In the very early days I was a loud mouth Christian. Some would argue I still am. I told people what had happened during the night I bowed the knee to Jesus and told them how life was now, now I knew the truth. It would be fair to say I received mixed responses. You have to remember that I had absolutely no Christian friends at this point, no one to converse with, pray with, discuss the faith with.

So I gave my testimony to work colleagues, friends and perhaps the hardest of all, my family. My brother had moved away from home, leaving me living with mum and dad at their house in Baildon.

Up until the point when I became a Christian, mum and dad, particularly mum, knew me better than anyone. They knew my quirks, my thoughts, my experiences, my personality, what made me tick, what got me angry, what made me laugh. Well, all that had changed.

I was a different person, now I knew Jesus, it wasn't just that I *wanted* to change things about myself, but the night I'd become a Believer, God took away certain aspects of my personality immediately. This must have been hard for mum and dad to see before their very eyes and I understand that fully. I didn't swear anymore and I used to have a complete potty mouth, I didn't blaspheme anymore, using God's name in vain or as a curse word. I stopped watching or reading certain things that I knew weren't helpful. I was completely committed to the Lord.

I lost friends, probably because they didn't recognize me anymore or didn't agree with my sudden change, some thought I had become a Christian for Jon, some thought I now believed myself to be somehow above everyone else. I was called a homophobe, a bigot, a weirdo, people were afraid I had joined a cult, they feared I was no longer tolerant of worldly issues and struggles. This couldn't be further from the truth.

I will say, that I have found that anybody who *isn't* a believer in Jesus Christ DOES NOT WANT to hear about Jesus Christ. About the grace of God. It's like trying to mix oil and water.

It might be interesting to know I changed physically in some ways too, toning my makeup, hair and clothing down as to not draw unnecessary attention to myself. I stopped drinking alcohol altogether, God instantly took away the need for something that gave me a false confidence. The cigarettes took a little longer to kick. But there was one thing I knew for sure that I had to do.

I knew I had to find a church.

I had spoken to Jon (my now husband) on the phone and told him about my conversion, he was absolutely thrilled and loved listening to my testimony. He'd been praying for my soul and God had answered those prayers. What a wonderful work of Grace. I asked him to look for a local church for me, where the teaching was sound, gospel teaching. He found Church on the Green, a small evangelical church at the bottom of Baildon Green, it was in an unassuming building I must have driven past so many times in my life without a second thought.

So I waved bye to mum and dad one Sunday morning and jumped in my car to go to church. To say I was nervous was an understatement. I was terrified. I had literally never set foot inside a church unless it was raining cats and dogs and I didn't want my hair to curl. So here I was, driving toward Church on the Green, a bible on my passenger seat and my heart pounding in my chest.

With the mentioning of my Bible on my passenger seat I would now like to review my earlier misconceptions. 1) It's no longer a dusty old, irrelevant tome to me, it's the wonderful word of God, it's a reliable, historical document chronicling life from the beginning and how God deals with his people through the ages. 2) Women in the Bible are not downtrodden and subservient, an example would be Eve, the 'mother of all living' who shows God's grace and mercy perfectly, she demonstrates the way he designed women for different accomplishments to men, they have different roles and share with man in equal measure; God's compassion, love, mercy and forgiveness. Other amazing women include; Abigail, Deborah, Ruth, Esther, Mary, Hannah, the list is actually exhaustive.

I passed the church. Instead of stopping and parking up, I continued to drive past. I'm still not sure why, looking back, I'm not sure why I was so hesitant to walk into this church. Perhaps Satan was exercising a final mocking and ridicule. People will laugh at me, I thought. They'll take one look at me and ask me to leave. They'll call me a fake. Satan continued to ridicule me as I drove past the church for the fifth time. Each time I would reach the end of the road, turn my car around and drive past it in the other direction. Maybe I would go next week? Once things died down a bit.

Then I pulled up in the tiny car park. Jesus wanted me to go into that church, so go into that church I must.

I pushed the door open. It didn't budge. I tried again. It refused to open. Maybe they locked it once everyone is in? I tried again, putting my whole weight against the door and heaving, but no avail. Then I realized there were two doors and I'd tried the wrong one. So I pulled the right one open and open it did...

I was welcomed by a man called Ray, he was tall and wore a suit. He spoke a few octaves lower than I'd heard before, greeting me with a warm smile and a Hymn book. Yes, I thought, this was it, this is where Jesus wanted me to be. I remember saying something along the lines of , 'Sorry, I've not been to church before, I don't know what to do.' He told me to sit with his wife, Barbara. Which one was Barbara??

I want to make this observation with the kindest of intentions, the majority of the congregation at Church on the Green was older, as in *retirement* age - older. There was nobody my age or younger, but that suited me just fine, because I've always got on with people of all ages and there was a warmth and experience alluding from them that made me feel instantly part of the family.

These were my first brothers and sisters In Christ and I instantly felt an affinity with them. The sermon was given by Pastor David, who shared a pastorate position with Ray. As I listened to the sermon, sang the hymns and prayed, I thought Yes! This is what I have been needing to hear! This is the spiritual food I have been craving since my conversion! Afterward I felt fulfilled and eager to hear more. I enjoyed coffee and cake and fellowship with my new family In Christ.

It might be helpful and amusing to note that the morning I entered Church on the Green for the first time, it was Baildon's famous Harley Davidson Weekend. Somewhere in the region of 200/300 bikers, donned leathers, boasted beards and tattoos and rode the most exquisite machines you've ever seen, gathered in Baildon village, taking over pubs, car parks and the village square. It's been a tradition of ours growing up, to go and see the bikes and later I learned that in the days leading up to that Sunday, Barbara, Ray's wife, had been praying that God would deliver some bikers to the morning service at Church on the Green.

No bikers showed up. But in walked a somewhat tarty looking girl, made up, hair done, heels on, no idea what to do. It's comforting to know that our prayers are answered by our loving God and not always in the way we expect. Praise the Lord!

And what an amazing way to encourage prayer! We just don't know what's happening all around us, but God does, our omnipresent God who is carefully and thoughtfully knitting together His plan, out of love for us, and for His Glory. I'm thankful that Barbara and the church were praying for people to walk in to a service. Hidden away on the bottom of Baildon Green, people seldom just walked into the church, and in my Christian experience over the years I've realised people seldom do any church. It takes prayer and commitment and trust on our part, and God will build His church.

I attended services regularly after that. I swapped my going out on the town for Wednesday night prayer meetings and bible studies. It wasn't that I had to, after all, it wasn't a requirement, but because I wanted to. I couldn't get enough of what Christian fellowship, worship and teaching had to offer. You can imagine, my mum and dad were confused to say the least and it did cause a rift and misunderstanding for a while, but nothing too big that God couldn't heal and make better.

Jon and I began a relationship. It's funny because Jon and I really are from completely different backgrounds and have lived significantly different lives. In my mind, we did not make a natural pairing, but this union was certainly arranged and blessed by God. He encouraged me in Christ, we read and studied together, I had continued to attend Church on the Green whilst he faithfully attended Mirfield Evangelical Church. Living a good forty minutes apart meant that I could grow as a Christian in my own time and not be swept up in a new relationship with a Christian man which would taint my young relationship with the Lord. I became a member of Church on the Green and was baptised. My baptism was a wonderful day, a day of showing people I loved, how committed I was to the Lord. It was a declaration and a symbol of my new birth In Christ. It was a well attended service, and due to the fact that I'd visited MEC many times for an evening service in the previous months, a lot of my Christian brothers and sisters who I now call dear friends came along to enjoy the day with me.

Jon and I attended many services at Church on the Green before our marriage, even taking a service one Sunday morning thanks to a suggestion from Pastor David, we did a reading and chose hymns and Jon played a Christian song he'd written on his guitar. It was a wonderful way to celebrate the Lord, to be able to get my teeth into the Bible, to choose a reading. What freedom and encouragement I received at that church, what great teaching and a wonderful foundation God built for me.

The date was set, Jon and I were to marry on November 3rd 2012, the service to be held at St Mary's Parish, Mirfield and the wedding reception at Oakwell Hall. It was a wonderful day of celebration and was attended by both our families, church families and friends. Getting married and moving to Mirfield saw my last service at Church on the Green in October 2012. It was a sad and reflective day but one of great promise and I was looking forward to joining the congregation at MEC and growing further in my Christian walk.

Mirfield Evangelical Church had a much larger membership and number of attendees. There were plenty of people my age and in similar situations ie young, married, working full time. I thank God for the important blessing of always placing me in the perfect church at the right time. Amen.

PART THREE
Living Life

Chapter 9
Rediscovering Christ after trauma

I don't want to kid myself that people reading this would want to know all the ins and outs of my life, either before I became a believer or after. The aim of this book really was to tell people about Christ and all he had done for me, after all, he commands it;

Acts 1:8, "But you will receive power when the Holy Spirit comes on you; and you will be my witnesses in Jerusalem, and in all Judea and Samaria, and to the ends of the earth."

What an honor!

Luke 8:39. 'Return home and tell how much God has done for you.' So the man went away and told all over town how much Jesus had done for him"

What a privilege!

And I am His now. He bought me with great cost (death on a cross) and I wish to tell people about the unfathomable Glory of God. Of His marvelous truths, the lengths that God goes to forgive us and welcome us back and the amazing ways this process plays out in people's lives. Everybody's testimonies are different, not all are as dramatic and intense as mine and some are significantly more dramatic (for a great story of God's grace in someone's life please read Ian McCormac's amazing testimony – 'A Glimpse of Eternity' the story of a man going from an atheist to a believer in a matter of minutes!)

Other testimonies I have heard include a gentle and wonderfully calm coming to the Lord. A simple trusting, perhaps an understanding from an early age that Jesus is The Way the Truth, the Life and that giving your heart to the Lord feels like a natural, effortless transaction. How wonderful my husband's testimony is, at six years old, knowing that he was a baddie in front of a goodie God. Therefore offered his heart (and his toys) to the Lord in an act of simple, beautiful humbleness. Knowing he deserved punishment and yet could come to our tender savoir who meets us where we are.

God knows each of us. There are no earthly requirements for being one of God's children and I hope that this book really accentuates that point.

However, in this part of the book I wanted to include a few details and happenings in my life in the years after my conversion. It could end now with the sentence, *'and they lived happily ever after...'* Which, in a sense, wouldn't be untrue. Because I have assurance In Christ, that I will be spending eternity with Him, which is the best *happily ever after* ever. But the journey, the way things play out for Christians on earth, on a daily basis, isn't always perfect.

God doesn't decide to shield us from trials and tribulations once we are believers. It's not some sort of pact between God and us that we inherit when we believe. But try telling me that a couple of years into my Christian walk.

Jon got ill just after we got married. It was a mystery at first, his body was just shutting down, his muscles, joints and bones cried out in pain, his lungs were damaged which affected his breathing. He could barely move, he couldn't climb stairs, he was swollen and in agony constantly. Eventually we got a diagnosis of Dermatomyositis (a auto immune connective tissue disorder) with no real cure. He underwent a program of treatment including steroids and intravenous chemotherapy, drugs used in cancer patients to destroy cells (all cells) in order to halt the condition. His condition is now under control but he continues to take heavy medication daily and have regular hospital visits. Its important to know one amazing thing about my husband and again, this is not just lip service; he never complains about anything, he never blames God for any pain or suffering, he continues to worship his saviour, he is such a lovely person.

I, on the other hand, remained fiery and immature at this stage of our lives. We'd just got married; we were excited about starting our life together, then Bam! Jon was really ill and it was a year until we got a diagnosis and treatment and even then it wasn't a quick fix.

So I threw my toys out of the pram. I did blame God. Why would he let this happen? Yeah, of course, everything is great when you're first converted, life seems simple and joyous and fulfilling, but a sinful world is still our earthly home, and we are not unsusceptible to disease and loss, challenges and difficulties. I didn't know this at first. I thought I'd be protected from all this by God. And I naively believed that if God kept me and the ones I loved safe, healthy and free from troubles, I could preach His greatness even better!

But that is NOT the Gospel message. That is NOT what Jesus preaches. That is NOT biblical.

So there I was, a young Christian, immature and moody, and basically shouting at God for not loving us enough to keep us from this horrendous situation. Boy, how sin and attitude can slip back in when our guard is down! Anger and reluctance to praise Him began to eat me up. I did feel bouts of depression, stress and anxiety and blamed God for the whole lot. He had the power to stop all this, I thought. And yet He's choosing to do nothing! Charming!

I was acting as if God was my personal physician or psychiatrist, able to help me, but choosing to take a leave of absence and let me muddle my own way through instead. It would be more than helpful to know that God never left my side during this time. I never once felt abandoned. Jesus walked with me everyday, even closer on the days that I wept and yelled and shouted.

A couple of years later I had a little girl, Elsie. Our first baby. Her birth was awful, traumatic for both me and her and in the weeks that followed, she contracted sepsis after a cold, she nearly died and I developed dangerously high blood pressure (preeclampsia). I spent time in hospital. I was separated from my baby a lot in the early weeks of her birth and again, I blamed God. This was more than I could handle. I cried a lot, developed acute anxiety disorder - which manifested itself in debilitating panic attacks in which I believed myself to be having a heart attack. I went to A+E so many times in the early months of Elsie's life, that I was almost on first name terms with the receptionists. I'd turn up, unable to breath, insisting I was having a heart attack, they would do blood tests and ECG tests and show me the results, proving to me that I wasn't dying, hours later I'd walk out and get a taxi home. I'd have another panic attack and lose the use of my arms, unable to raise them and my speech, unable to form words properly, which was terrifying and those who witnessed it were horrified. This was my life for eight months before I got help.

I'd pushed God further and further away. I professed to trust Him, but I didn't really believe that in my heart anymore, I was too damaged, too scared, the responsibility of a baby and the affect it had had on my body and mind was too much for me to push aside all of that and focus on Jesus Christ. I grew further away. I found it hard to sing the hymns at church. I couldn't rejoice. I couldn't praise.

I was too anxious. I had no control, and that scared me, yet I wasn't willing to trust God with the control of my life. I wanted to try and keep a handle on everything.

I made myself ill. I ended up on medication.

Two Christian sisters stepped in in October 2015. Elsie was eight months old and I was really in a bad way. They put me in touch with a Christian counsellor called Ian, who visited Dewsbury Evangelical Church once a month. I agreed to go and I think my opening words to Ian was, when we met, 'there's nothing you can tell me about myself that I don't already know.'

His reply had been a sincere, 'But there *are* things about God that you do not know or have forgotten.'

No truer words had been spoken. I'd forgotten or chosen to ignore God's great love and promises. I had pushed aside Christ and tried to control life myself, in my own strength, I blamed God, in fact, I was angry with God for saving me! I recall saying something like, it would have been easier for me to deal with challenges if I was still living in my ignorance, at least then I wouldn't have anyone to blame but myself when things went wrong!

How distorted my view had become.

God's goodness no longer meant anything to me, or if it did, it was buried too far down and I had piled a heap of trash and garbage on top of it, suffocating it. But God is not so easily pushed aside. Praise the Lord!

I had expected my sessions with Ian to be all about *me*, like 'normal' counseling is, when in fact they were all about God. He took me back to my salvation In Christ, my rebirth. He taught me about who God was, all my questions and accusations were answered wonderfully by faithful bible reading and prayer. This verse from Galatians explains it perfectly;

"Are you so foolish? After beginning with the spirit, are you now trying to attain your goal by human effort?" **Galatians 3:3**

I had sessions with Ian for a year, a wonderful year, God used that year to teach me who He was, that Christ was right beside me, that He was in control and worthy of being trusted with that control. I didn't need to panic. God is the alpha and omega, he is light and love and His Word tells us that he is an almighty God, that I can trust in Him. That I *could* and *should* live with confidence and assurance.

Psalm 23:4 Even though I walk through the valley of the shadow of death, I fear no evil, for You are with me; Your rod and Your staff, they comfort me.

I praise God that he never let me go, he allowed me to go through those trials to richen my relationship with Him. I'm not exempt from disaster or challenges, I'm susceptible to anxiety and worry and doubt, but being a new creation In Christ, means I should approach it differently to how I would have done before, God allowed me time to learn this, to *really* learn it, until it sunk deep into my bones and became part of me, to fully trust, to fully love and worship.

Praise the Lord.

Chapter 10
The Glory of God

When I talk about that year of my life I always smile. Which is strange because it was excruciating and terrifying at the time. But I learnt so much about God it was a privilege to live through it. A sermon was preached in the following January by the Pastor from DEC, I was sitting on the front row and rejoicing, it was about fruits of the spirit, about the vine about bearing fruit and being more like Christ. My notes from that sermon include the lines; Character and conduct is fruit and will only grown in accordance with commitment to Christ.

Since that year, I have continued to grow In Christ. I'm not perfect, but the One I cling to is perfection personified.

The last few years have brought amazing blessings and trials. Two years after having Elsie, I suffered a miscarriage. It was horrendous and painful and humiliating. I lost my baby at almost twelve weeks, and the moment the doctors confirmed that for me, a wonderful truth occurred to me, I can trust God with this.

Scripture confirmed this;

Joshua 1:9 "Have I not commanded you? Be strong and courageous. Do not be frightened, and do not be dismayed, for the Lord your God is with you wherever you go."

Isaiah 41:10 "Fear not, for I am with you; be not dismayed, for I am your God; I will strengthen you, I will help you, I will uphold you with my righteous right hand."

Zephaniah 3:17 "The Lord your God is in your midst, a mighty one who will save; he will rejoice over you with gladness; he will quiet you by his love; he will exult over you with loud singing."

Psalm 147:3 He heals the brokenhearted and binds up their wounds.

Romans 5:8 'but God shows his love for us in that while we were still sinners, Christ died for us."

It's not just the significance of the loss or challenge, but it's a deeper understanding of the love of Christ that gives our hearts the means to understand these things. Of course I was heartbroken, but its nothing Jesus Christ hasn't felt before, to a greater magnitude, of course I was in pain and upset, but again, it wasn't anything that Christ hadn't himself felt whilst dying for me on the cross.

On losing a baby I experienced the opposite reaction to how I responded to trials and sadness in previous years. I'd learnt so much about God, I'd immersed myself in his teachings and his truths and I truly believed them. He would get me through this. His hand would hold me up. I lost my baby on the Thursday and was in church on the Sunday, worshipping the Lord our God. I was sad, I was crying, but I was rejoicing.

For He is truly worthy of worship. He doesn't owe me anything, he has already performed the ultimate act of pure love and forgiveness in sending His Son to die on the cross that we might spend eternity with him. What else did we want?? An abundance of earthly blessings? Perfect day to day life? A bigger house? A lottery win??

Jesus Christ is the ultimate treasure. The ultimate gift.

On the following Wednesday I'd agreed to visit Ian (Counsellor Ian) at Dewsbury because he had a lady coming to speak with him about her struggle with anxiety, not too dissimilar to my earlier struggle, I didn't cancel my meeting with them. I went. I informed them I'd lost my baby a few days earlier but I wanted to be there. I wanted to tell her my story, how the Lord has dealt with me, lifted me up, taught me his truths. How anxiety didn't govern my life, how I learnt to let go and completely trust In Him.

And God blessed the days and weeks that followed. It remains to this day, my most active stretch of giving people the Gospel of Christ. I could truly speak and gush of His love and faithfulness, you might be reading this now and remember that time and perhaps you were somebody I spoke to about the Lord. I hope you are. Because God wanted me to.

And that's bigger than us and our lives and opinions.

Psalm 46

1 God is our refuge and strength, an ever-present help in trouble. **2** Therefore we will not fear, though the earth give way and the mountains fall into the heart of the sea, **3** though its waters roar and foam and the mountains quake with their surging. **4** There is a river whose streams make glad the city of God, the holy place where the Most High dwells. **5** God is within her, she will not fall; God will help her at break of day. **6** Nations are in uproar, kingdoms fall; he lifts his voice, the earth melts. **7** The LORD Almighty is with us; the God of Jacob is our fortress. **8** Come and see what the LORD has done, the desolations he has brought on the earth. **9** He makes wars cease to the ends of the earth. He breaks the bow and shatters the spear; he burns the shields with fire. **10** He says, "Be still, and know that I am God; I will be exalted among the nations, I will be exalted in the earth." **11** The LORD Almighty is with us; the God of Jacob is our fortress.

Chapter 11
Living faithfully

My son, Edward, came along in December 2017, his birth much better than Elsie's but I was battling pneumonia at the time and felt very weak. Again, the Lord was gracious. On recovering, I was once again struck by how life is endlessly rewarding In Christ; I'm free to go to church and worship the God I love, which in itself is a blessing as there are so many areas in this world where following Jesus is a dangerous and life threatening activity. I am blessed with a wonderful husband, two gorgeous children, great parents and a loving, supportive church family.

I am used in His service - which is a privilege. I attend and help out at the church's toddler groups, Sunday schools, bible studies and various evangelistic events. I love talking to other mums about Christ and always feel greatly fortunate to be able to witness and give my testimony. Every opportunity is a blessing.

So here we are, back at the beginning of my book, sitting in church having sung And Can It Be. The sermon is on the spotless Lamb of God. He is Flawless. And that is the perfect title for my book. Flawless. Without blemish. Perfect. The Lord Jesus Christ. Our Hope and Saviour.

Reflecting on the journey of my life, I am so grateful that God's grace is inexhaustible, and I am just one person! There are so many Christians out there for whom he is just the same, a faithful, loving Father. He never tires and He went to extraordinary lengths to show that love.

Jesus is Lord.

9 781913 247119